Niotaze, Kansas

**Indians, Slavery, the Civil War,
Robbers, Land Runs, Pioneers,
Orphan Trains, Oil, Gold,
Schools**

The state of Kansas is named after the Kansas River which runs through it which in turn was named after the **Kansa Native American Indian Tribe** which inhabited the area. The tribe's name is said to mean **'people of the wind'** or **'people of the south wind'.** They later added 's' to Kansa making it Kansas.

Kansas was called **'Bleeding Kansas'** because the **Abolitionists** who were called **'Jay Hawkers'** fought fiercely for the freedom and rights of slaves and had an underground railroad for runaway slaves to hide in until it was safe to go farther north into other states and Canada where there was no slavery.

Slavery and the Great Civil War

People with money were coming to the young America and buying slaves to build their mansions, and work the very large farms.
The black slaves were being rounded up and kept in chains until the slave ships came and then their chiefs would sell them and they were taken by boat to America and sold to the highest bidder. A black slave could cost eight hundred dollars.

Also there were over 300,000 'white slaves' who were Irish women, men, and children who were rounded up in Britain by King James and Cornwall and sold into slavery by Britain and taken by ships to America and other countries and sold. They sold for a much cheaper price than the black slaves as they were more plentiful.

King James and Cornwall found 'white slavery' a quick and easy way to get money and raided their villages often.

For discipline 'whipping' was a popular way to keep black slaves obedient. Since the Irish slaves were much cheaper and plentiful to obtain, a popular way to keep them obedient was tying one up by the hands and setting their hands and feet on fire burning them alive then putting their skull on a stake for everyone to see.
I found in history burning prisoners and slaves were common.

Many of these Irish women and young girls were forced to 'breed' with black slaves to obtain a more docile person that would submit easier to their masters. They were called 'mulattoes.' .

There were also people brought from Italy and sold as slaves and were also treated poorly and were called 'Whops'

Also many Native Indians were made into slaves. They also were in abundant supply and were many times worked to death as there was a plentiful supply to replace them with.
I was told the Spanish were notorious for this practice also.

I read that the Irish was of the Catholic faith and religious and though much cheaper to buy the slave owners preferred the black slaves because they were not Christian.
They thought by bringing the black slaves to America they were 'Christianizing' them bringing them to a better way of life.

John Newton was a British slave ship Captain and slave trader who led a prosperous life.

One night returning home with his ship full of human cargo a severe storm rose up and thinking he was going to die he prayed. He gave up his trade and became active in the **Abolition** movement and also became a minister and wrote the beautiful song ' **Amazing Grace'** 200 years ago!
He became friends with a rising star in parliament named **William Wilberforce** and **Slavery was made illegal in Britain in 1807.**

Harriet Beecher Stowes, Author of 'Uncle Tom's Cabin' in 1859 was an active **Abolitionist** and also a teacher at the Heartford Female Academy in Connecticut.

She wrote the book **'Uncle Tom's Cabin'** telling the plight of slavery while being assertive that **Christian Love** can overcome something that is as destructive as slavery being done to our fellow human beings.

The book sold hundreds of thousands of copies, being the second best seller to **The Holy Bible** in the 19th. century and it greatly inflamed the **Abolitionists** cause in the 1850's.

When Abraham Lincoln first met Miss Harriet Beecher Stowes he exclaimed " So this is the little lady who started the great war!"

'Uncle Tom's Cabin' was written in part of remembrances of Josiah Henson.

In 1830 Josiah Henson, a former slave, escaped fleeing to Ontario. He had worked on a 3,700 acres tobacco farm in Maryland.
He would help other slaves escape and train them a trade so they could support themselves.
His cabin was torn down but the Maryland Museum got another one he might have lived in for display

.

John Brown May 9, 1800-Dec. 2, 1859

A Kansan, John Brown, a **Puritan Abolitionist**, was five years old when he and his father visited a farm in Ohio and saw a slave severely beaten and the horror of it never left his mind throughout his life.

His father, a **Puritan,** despised slavery teaching him that God hated slavery and one person is not to own another.

Quakers believed all colors and races were equal in the eyes of God.

Both **Abolitionists and Republicans** were very much against slavery but they tried to be peaceful about the work of 'freeing these slaves' but the peaceful talks were not working.

In other countries also people were buying and using slaves for labor and it was a **'class statement'** as black slaves cost a lot of money to buy and only the rich could afford to buy them.

Many of the politicians and government officials owned slaves:

Presidents and Slavery 1789-1877

George Washington 1789-1797 Va. had 18 slaves of his own and inherited 200 more when he married.
(Is said to have fathered a boy child with a 15 year old slave girl in a friends home.)

John Adams 1797-1801 Mass. Received one slave that cooked.

Thomas Jefferson 1801-1809 Va. Wife had a dowry of 100 slaves and he bought many more. He is said to be the biggest slave owner.
In 1798 he owned 141 slaves, many of them elderly.

One of his slaves was a half sister to his diseased wife.
When his daughter married he gave her 1000 acres and 25 slaves.

James Madison 1809-1817 Va. He sold several farms but none of his slaves. A year later he sold 16 slaves to a relative with their permission.

James Monroe 1817-1825 Va. He owned 30 or 40 slaves plus one named Ralph.

John Quency Adams 1825-1829 Mass. He owned no slaves.

Andrew Jackson 1829-1837 S.C. He may have had at least 300 slaves and his businesses included Slave Trading.

Martin Van Burin 1837-1841 N.Y. Had 1 slave named Tom.

William Henry Harrison 1841 Va. He had 7 slaves. Slavery became illegal where he lived so he made 'indentured servants' of them. He tried to make slavery legal in Indiana but failed.

John Tyler 1841-1845 Va. Did not own slaves.

James K. Polk 1845-1849 N.C. Had 15 slaves. He said whippings were feared more than imprisonment and it had a beneficial effect on fellow slaves.

Zachary Taylor 1849-1850 Va. Had over 100 slaves.

Millard Fillmore 1830-1853 N.Y. He had no slaves. He detested slavery.

Franklin Pierce 1853-1837 N.H. Had no slaves.

James Buckanan 1857-1861. P. A. He bought two slaves from his brother in law and made them indentured servants till they were 28 and 29 years old.

Abraham Lincoln 1861-1865 Ky. O slaves. Stated when he heard anyone that was for slavery he thought it should be tried on that person personally.

Andrew Johnson 1865-1869 N.C. Had nine slaves and the Confederates confiscated them and they got free and came home and he made 'freemen' of them.
He stated " **Have you thought of the millions of the White**

Southern people who have been liberated by the war!!
(meaning the white slaves)

Ulyssis S. Grant 1869-1877. Ohio. He had owned 1 slave and his wife had been given 200 slaves by her father as a wedding gift.

The rich had the money to pay for attorneys, and to sponsor politicians running for powerful government positions.

John Brown

John Brown stated slavery was so 'entrenched' in the young America that this 'talking and peaceful means' was not going to make slavery come to a stop!
He believed slavery could only be destroyed by violent means.

John Brown and his sons moved to **Kansas** to support the **'Free Soil Settlers'** who wanted Kansas to come into the Union a 'free state' where slavery would be outlawed.

He spoke to run away slaves and other **Abolitionists** and decided change was not going to happen unless it was done by force!!

John Brown talked with runaway slaves, other Abolitionists, and to two newspaper editors and believed slavery was so ingrained in the U.S. that armed resurrectionists was the only way to over throw the institution of slavery out of the United States.

In 1856 John Brown commanded his sons and some volunteer forces at the Battle of Black Jack and the Battle of Osawatomie, Kansas.

He also killed 5 pro-slavery supporters at Pottawatomie.

In 1859 he led a successful raid on the Federal Armory at Harpers Ferry, Virginia. He had planned to rob the arsenal for guns and ammunition and arm the runaway slaves and start a guerrilla war in the south with guns and strategy.

December 2, 1859 (155 years ago) John Brown was captured and sentenced to death with 4 of his men by hanging for treason against the common wealth of Virginia in Charleston.

The **Abolitionist** gained a Martyr and the execution of John Brown was a step on the countries' **road to Civil War.'**

John Brown believed he was the 'Instrument of God's wrath' in punishing men for the sin of owning slaves.

John Brown played major roles in ending slavery as a Martyr.

Song: John Brown's Body

This song made him a heroic martyr and was a popular song during the civil war.

It was a popular 'marching' song for men to sing while marching.

John Brown's Body Lyrics

John Brown body lies a mouldering in the grave
His soul is marching on

Chorus:

Glory glory halleluiah   Glory glory halleluiah
His soul is marching on His soul is marching on

He's gone to be a soldier in the army of the Lord
His soul is marching on

John Brown's knapsack is strapped upon his back
His soul is marching on

His pet lambs will meet him on the way
They will go marching on

They will hang **Jeff Davis** to a sour apple tree
As they go marching on

Now three rousing cheers for the Union
As they go marching on

From the library of congress published 1861

(Re: **Jeff Davis**-Jefferson Davis was elected President of the Southern States Feb.-22-1862 to May-10-1865. He was captured in 1865 for treason and spent 2 years in prison and let go without a trial.)

John Brown and his sons and volunteers and other anti slavery people plus several 'run away slaves' pushed the country into the great Civil War after he was hung for treason as a Martyr.

Some called him a **'terrorist'**

In **Niotaze Grade School** we learned about **John Brown** the **Abolitionist** in our History books and in classes and he was a Hero giving his life to help free the slaves. 1955

Some Slave Owners Who Became Infamous Outlaws:

The slave owners who fought to keep slavery were called **'Bush Whackers'**. The two groups fought each other fiercely in both Kansas and MO. shedding much blood in Kansas and the state was called **'Bleeding Kansas'** because of the bloodshed.
   William Quantrill, Jessie and Frank James, Belle Star, and the **Younger Bros.** families were rich slave owners living in MO. which fought and were considered **'Bushwhackers.'**
   After the war was over with their homes destroyed, their money stolen, and many of their family members murdered they became **outlaws and robbers.**
   Frank and Jesse James' father had been a preacher with a nice church and had went to California to the gold mines to teach the miners about Jesus and died with a virus he had caught there.
   Their mother had married a school teacher and they owned slaves.
   Union soldiers tortured their beloved stepfather trying to force him to tell where his step son Frank was.
   Jesse walked from a field where he had been plowing in time to see the soldiers who had tied a rope around a tree limb in the front yard and put a noose around the step father's throat and swung him back and forth injuring his neck and throat then put him in jail in another town.
   The step father was a school teacher and after his cruel treatment he could barley utter his words as his vocal chords were injured and his neck had been greatly injured.
In his community he was well liked and respected.

The Younger family was rich and had slaves then one day on his way to town, their father was ambushed, robbed, and murdered. Their family home and buildings were burned down. The boys got their mother and whatever they could salvage and headed for Texas.

The Younger's and Jesse and Frank James were cousins and Belle Shirley were friends with them and they went to school together.

William Quantrill was born into privilege and was a school teacher.

Belle Shirley's father John Shirley was the judge and ran a tavern.
Belle played the piano there and sang and also at church on Sundays.
Both the Union and Confederate soldiers would stop in at the tavern and share the news as they drank and listened to Belle playing the piano and singing.
Belle's brother was a Confederate soldier and Belle was a spy listening to the Union soldiers and passing on information to her brother.
John Shirley also owned slaves, a boarding house with a livery stable, and farmed the land that he owned.
The Union soldiers killed Belle's brother and started burning homes and businesses so hurriedly Belle's father sold his tavern, stable, rooming house, home, land, and whatever and gathered what money he could get together and headed for Texas before they were burned out also.
In Texas they lived in a dug out until the father could build a two room house. He tried to rebuild what he had left behind but he was getting older. No southerners were allowed to hold a public job under this Union government.

The Younger brothers, and Frank and Jesse would visit and stay with the Shirleys' then travel back through Kansas stopping to visit on their travels.

Belle's mother was a Hatfield who came from the Hatfields' and McCoys.
Belle was sent to a private school and excelled in her studies and excelled in the art of playing the piano.
When in prison for horse theft she stayed with the warden and home schooled his children.
When she was released the warden, his wife and children would Send her boxes of fresh fruit at Christmas time.
When she was released she played the piano for the famous **Hanging Judge Parker.**
Gene Autry is said to have been her cousin and her famous pearl handled pistol is said to be in the museum he owned.
Belle married one of the Younger brothers in **Baxter Springs**, Kansas when the war was over.
Belle Shirley later married Sam Starr and became the infamous **Belle Starr.**

Jessie James would stop at Cascade Community to eat, visit,

and freshen up on his way to **Sam and Belle Starr's** home in **Indian Territory** in Oklahoma.

It is said Belle Starr and the Dalton Boys were well known in Elgin when it was a big cow town and also at Cascade, both border towns.

A man who lives in Coffeyville says he is **Jesse James' grandson** and has inherited some family things. He states Jesse was never killed, that another man had taken his place.

In 1882 the **Dalton Boys** put Coffeyville, Kansas in the news when they tried to rob two banks at the same time and **Henry Starr** of Nowata, Oklahoma robbed the Tyro, Kansas Bank and put Tyro, Kansas in the news.

I am adding that the outlaws came to Kansas before and after the Civil War ended and is part of our history.

The **Civil War** was over with Kansas a Free State and #34 to join the **Union** which became the **United States of America**.

Abolitionists had blended with the **Republican** Party and fought to have Kansas a free state. When the war was over the former slaves were given parcels of land and started successful businesses and some went on the become politicians as they raised their families and served their country.

From the **Irish slaves (white slaves)** I read many of the Irish that were rounded up and sold had been involved in heated politics of the day.

President John F. Kennedy was Irish and his father, his brothers and family were into politics and his father's family came from Ireland.

The Kennedys' usually ran on the Democrat ticket.

The **Bushwhackers** who wanted to keep slavery went on to start the **K.K.K** it is said and to be democratic and wanting to control the former slaves through threats and intimidation.

The K.K.K. is still in place but now instead of using fear and intimidation it promises **free stuff and favors for their votes at election time if they are elected to office such as more welfare, food stamps and free cell phones etc. as their own bank accounts grow.** (The poor get poorer and the rich gets richer)

Earlier several thousands of Native American Indians had been moved to Kansas from their homes in other states then later moved to Oklahoma. On the land given to the Osage Indians much **oil** was found and many of them became **wealthy.**

Starting in 1854 Kansas started opening up for settlements and different sizes of parcels of land were given out or sold cheaply to those who would homestead and farm the land or build ranches.

Many people came from other countries to settle and many others moved from the eastern states going west for the **Homestead Acts and Land Runs.**

There are remains of two 'Sod Houses' that were built by settlers to live in while they built homes to live in left over from earlier times in Chautauqua, Ks..

Because of the many rain falls, high humidity, flat ground, and high winds constantly blowing , many people thought Kansas was undesirable saying **only 'Robbers and Trappers would live there.**

Chautauqua County Kansas has rich sandy soil that has many natural springs of fresh water oozing to the surface. Black Jack Oak trees grows plentiful and is a natural habitat for all kinds of wild life such as deer, wolves, coyotes, snakes, wild turkeys, wild hogs, whippoorwills, panthers, bob cats, and snakes. Gold has been found here also!

My grandfather A.C. Cooper came here from Rose, Illinois in a covered wagon with his parents when he was 2 years old in the 1800's. They settled in Chautauqua County.
He and many others always had **traps** set and would sell the fur. In an old Sedan newspaper put on microfilm they said he had killed more wolves than anyone else that year and had saved a lot of livestock.

****

To Fill The Land

The Children's Aid Society of New York gathered homeless and orphaned children who were mostly living on the streets and put them on trains calling them **'Orphan Trains'** The trains would stop at scheduled stops and have the children get out and line up along the side of the train and people would come and chose the child or children they desired and took them home. The children who had not been chosen were put back on the train and taken to other scheduled stops hoping someone would want them. **One hundred fifty thousand children** rode on those orphan trains and Kansas residents chose to keep **five thousand** of them.

Jay Hawk, Kansas

The first settlement town in Chautauqua County was named '**Jay Hawk**' in 1870 then changed to '**Montanzas**' in 1871 with William R. Jones as the post master. It had a trading post or General Store with a Post Office owned by W. L. Williams and W. D. Nance, a Grist Mill, and a Black Smith Shop owned by Cal Robison and George Tames. It had a one room school house named Jay Hawk School started in 1879.

One room schools were built two and three miles apart so children would be able to walk or ride their horses and be able to attend school.

In **1886** The **Santa Fe Rail Road and the Pacific Rail Road** were built and missed their town. Cal Robison bought the General Store owned by W. D. Nance then sold it to George Tames who moved it two blocks north of the present highway 166 and closer to the two rail road tracks and two depots.

Niotaze, Kansas

In 1887 they named this community '**Niota**' but there was a mix up with Neola, Kansas. Then the community named it **New Port** but there was a New Port Kentucky and the abb. Ks. And Ky. was similar and caused confusion and Mr. Gorby was post master then. Mr. Huffman became postmaster and renamed the community **Niota and added 'ze'** to it and it has been '**Niotaze**' since.

W. D. Nance owned the Store with the Post Office and the Post Master was William H. Jones.

The first resident of Niotaze was J. E. Edwards who lived on the west hill and near his house was a school said to be a log cabin called **Walnut Valley School** which children came from a wide area to attend. No school census was kept. School houses were also used for church and community gatherings.

Taken from the Horoscope   May 25, 1894

I. O. G. T. (Independent Order of Good Templars) Lodge

Chief Templar,	George Smith
Vice Templar,	Mrs. Klinger
Supt. Juvenile Templar,	Lena Harris
Recording Secretary,	Denton Stone
Assistant Secretary,	J. B. Wilson
Financial Secretary,	J. D. Hampton
Treasurer,	Ethel Dobbs
Past Chief Templar,	Harry Patterson
Chaplain,	Mr. Dobbs
Marshall,	Henry Abbott
Deputy Marshall,	Lela Hart
Inside Guard,	Theron Stone
Outside Sentinel,	Charlie Keeling
Lodge Deputy,	H. J. Gregory

The Peru Lodge visited Wednesday evening.
The Chief Templar of Brooklyn, New York
visited the Lodge Thursday night.

Some names and dates I come across.

1920's   Rebekah Lodge # 286

Mrs. Emma Bartley
Mrs. G.B. Beeson
Lydia Bowles
Adaline Bowman
Lyda Beeson
J. Jeeson
Elisa E. Benson
Gladys Cobb
Mary Cobb
Daisy D. Crain
Nellie Ferrell
Viola Ferrell
Bessie E. Fry
Stella Griggs
T.J. Hatfield
Mrs. Jennie Henderson
Jennie Kelly

Ethel Legon
Mrs. Grace Mc Lain
Mrs. G.M. Morris
George M. Norris
Dan Pinnell
Martie Pinell
Frank Rayl
Mrs. Frank Rayl
Harry Rayl
Mrs. Myrtle Roberts
Mr. Roberts
Edna Rowe
Adaline Sanders
G.O. Sanders
Mrs. Guy Sanders
Pearl Sanders
Mrs. J.B. Stafford
Maude Scott
Lela E. Shannon
B. Wilson
Nettie Wilson
Stella Wilson
Nellie Williams
Mrs. Woodmancie

Rebekah Lodge 1.0.0.F #286

1921
Daisy Crain
Mary Cobb
Gladys Cobb

1922
Mrs. Guy Sanders
Mrs. Emma Bartley
Mrs. Ruth Bowles
Mrs. Grace Mc Clain
Mrs. G.B. Beeson
Mrs. Myrtle Roberts
Bessie E. Fry
Mrs. T.J. Stafford
B.D. Wilson
Mrs. Daisy Crain
Nellie Williams
Mrs. Jennie Henderson
G. O. Sanders

George M. Norris
Frank Rayl
Mrs. Frank Rayl
Harry Rayl
Mrs. Harry Rayl
Nellie Williams
Stella Wilson
Stella Griggs
Lydia Bowles
Adaline Sanders
Anna N. Hampton
Stella Wilson
Daisy Crain

Jan. 14, 1935
Stella Griggs
Lydia Bowles
Adaline Sanders
Anna N. Hampton
Stella Wilson
Daisy Crain
Nellie Williams

Aug. 27, 1941
Daisy Crain
Stella Wilson
Nellie Wilson

Niotaze Sunflower Band Members
(With picture)

1st row-
Fred Hocket
Roy Hocket
Frank Finney
Roy Hampton
Jesse Wright
Otton Henderson
Windom Hinder
Lyle Tame
Albert Hocket

2nd. Row
Arthur Bessy
Charles Flautt
Jay Knapp

John Bushwell
Latte Crandell

3rd. row
Ralph Perkins
James Shouse
George Guy
Root Mason
Newton Rayl
Elmer Kirkendal
Amos DuBois

Education and Schools

The first school was a log cabin named '**Walnut Valley School**' west of town. No records were kept.

In 1879 records show there were 52 pupils holding class in a one room frame building.

In 1880 records show school was in session 12 weeks and total expenditure for year was $89.84 for the term.

The first document to record the teacher was made July 1881. G.S. Hamilton was contracted to teach a 12 week term for a salary of $28.00 per month.

In 1884 the district was known as Little Cana. Miss Carrie Sterns, teacher, opened a 4 month term of school on April 7, at a salary of $25.00 per month.

Also in the records it was found that the teacher of the 3 previous terms Mr. Hamilton had been appointed as clerk of the district by County Superintendent Magga Kilmer.

In 1899 a large two story frame school house was built and it included a two year high school.

In 1939 a large cement school was built through a federal work program, W.PA. labor (Work Program Association) and it had 2 class rooms and a multipurpose basement.

Description of the school: it is made of concrete, modern in design and equipment. Two classrooms, a library, and a teacher's room are on the ground floor and the basement is a combined recreation and lunch room. A complete kitchen with an adjoining room filled with a variety of canned and stored foods is an important part of equipment. One end of the basement is furnished as a stage with hard wood floors and proper lighting. The entire building is equipped with fluorescent lights and heated with built in gas heaters. Windows are shaded by venation blinds.

The Dedication

November 13, 1942 The principal of the school: Miss Marie Bruce and the Niotaze School district presided at a program which opened with the audience singing "America". The 5 pupils of the school representing all 8 grades sang the Marine Hymn and 'The Cassions Go Rolling Along'.
Mrs. Clara Eddie, county superintendent, attended.
W.L. Rayl, clerk of the school board read the letter from the architect who designed the building expressing regret at not being able to attend the dedication. T.N. Millard, principal of the Sedan High School made a timely address.
Miss Earline Lemert, teacher of the lower grades expressed words of appreciation to the school patrons. Charles Scott made a brief talk to which William A. Patterson, director of the school responded.
B.D. Wilson, an early resident of Niotaze vicinity spoke on the changes that had taken place since he has lived there.
C.A. Moon, treasurer of the school board, gave a report on a garden project participated with 10 other schools of the county have sponsored a 5 acre garden and provided many hundreds of cans of vegetables as well as quantities of potatoes, carrots, and other vegetables which are used to provide nourishing meals for the pupils of the schools taking part.

Consolidations

In 1946 the one room schools **Cascade, Jay Hawk, Birch Creek, Otter Creek and part of Hillsdale** was consolidated into the **Niotaze School District #90.**
Students were bussed from and to their homes by two busses.

In 1950 a two room school was built which housed the two lower grades.

In 1966 the Niotaze School System was consolidated into the Caney Valley School System in M.G. county.

Lunch Time
In the cement school

At lunch grades one through four went over to the cement school and stood in lines in the hall way and marched down the steps to the basement for dinner and set at long tables.

Then the four upper grades also formed lines in the hall and did the same.

When the children were through eating they could go outside for recess.

After lunch and noon recess, the teachers would sometimes read 'fairy tales' as the pupils laid they heads on the desks.

Some of the cooks I remember are Ruth Bowles with Mrs. Brown and in the late 1950's Mrs. James Lumley (Dorothy) who did not want a helper.
She was a very good cook making us home made doughnuts and would teach us to play chords on the piano.

The stage was in the basement with the piano where the 'community meetings' were held. There was a stage with a purple blue curtain.

Dorothy Lumley went on to college and became a Home Ec. Teacher in the Coffeyville School System. Her husband was a farmer and a school bus driver and their son Jimmy attended school there also.

Farming

The Little Caney River bottoms were rich farm land and Niotaze became a prosperous farming community. W.J. Williams and John R. Dodson were well known farmers.

In the beginning several had raised cotton and it became unprofitable later on and they went on to other ventures.
It is written today Kansas is one of the most productive agricultural states producing high yields of wheat, sorghum, and sunflowers

Early Niotaze

There were three grocery stores, three doctor's offices, a dentist office, 'The Horoscope Newspaper, a meat market, an ice house, a green house, a barber shop, a pool hall, a livery stable, two depots, two grain elevators, two stock pens, a drug store, The Long Bell Lumber Company, a picture gallery, a bank, The Burson Hotel, a Lodging House, three churches, The Sunflower State Refinery, and several other businesses not listed.

There were some people who had businesses in both Caney and Niotaze and traveled between the two towns.

Fairview Cemetary

The Niotaze Fairview Cemetery was organized in 1909.
No records were kept. All members paid one dollar.
Members and directors held suppers for money to support their work.

July 5, 1913 **G.W. Bowen** sold the cemetery board 2 acres of land for $100.00 to expand the present cemetery. On April 9, 1922 the owner of the land at the time **L.A. Lockwood** donated a strip of land o the east side of the county road for parking space.

The main gate was erected in 1932 by the **1.0.0.F. Lodge No. 438** in memory of brothers and sisters.

The committee of the Lodge were: **George N. Crane, George C. Dye, L. S. Mathers, Alvin T. Sanders, Ben D. Wilson, and Joe H. Wilson.**

May 11 1937 the property of the Fairview Cemetery Ass. was transferred to the taxing district. There are 43 square miles in the district.

May 27, 1937 The taxing district was organized to elect the directors. The directors of the old association who resigned were: President **Earl Riggs**, Vice president **J.A. Henderson**, trustees: **Everett Henderson, William A. Patterson, Joe Wilson, George Dodson and A.D. Nance**. Secretary : **Edna Rowe** Treasurer: **Nellie Williams.** Sexton: **B.D. Wilson.**

The new taxing district was called The Fairview Cemetery District 3 and 5 directors were elected: President **J.A. Henderson,** and directors : **William A. Patterson, Earl Riggs, George Dodson, and Everett Henderson. Edna Row** was elected secretary, **Nellie Williams** as treasurer, and **B.D. Wilson** as sexton.

The new taxing district included 5 cemeteries. The main cemetery is **Fairview Cemetery, Ireland Cemetery, Whitten Cemetery, Otter Creek Cemetery**, and **P.M. Cemetery**.

On March 11, 1941 The Fairview Cemetery Board voted to dedicate a page in secretaries to **Edna Row** who had been secretary for 29 years when she passed away December 11, 1940. A picture of **Edna L. Rowe** and her home is on the same page.

July 9, 1962 **C.E. Chamberlain** donated and deeded an acre of land across the road on the east side for expansion. It is called **"The Chamberlain Addition"**.

August 16, 1971 the estate of **Nellie Williams** donated $2,000.00 for the construction of restrooms and 2 storage sheds.

Jan. 7, 1983 **Stephen R. Shaffer** donated one acre of land across the road and north of the Chamberlain Addition.

Directors who have served from 1937 are: **J.A. Henderson, B.D. Wilson, William A. Patterson, George Dodson, Earl Riggs, Everett Henderson, Lizzie Henderson, N.H. Rayl, Jim Greer, Ellis Patterson, Ira Guier, Q.C. Henderson, Ira Fulton, L.S. Mathers, James Barnhart, Leonard Farner, Robert Rayl, Floyd Haines, John Gragg, Benton Flesher, Ray Guier, Neil smith, Ed Houser, Fred Carra, Harold Sullivan, Dan Scott, George Boggs, W.L. Rayl, Bob Henderson, Juanita Artherton, Lottie Haines, Clark Benson, Earl Nance, John Dodson, Jim Rink, and R.C. Dye. They were elected for one year each.**

The present directors are: president: **Bob Henderson**, Sec. and treasurer**: Jim Rinck**.

Members: **Clark Benson, George Boggs, and R.C. Dye** members. Members are elected to 4 year terms.

By: 1981 **Bob Henderson**

Captain Joseph Jasper Stone

I have names but not too much on early settlers lives and what they did to earn a living. There were farmers and store owners and employees but I found this gentleman, **Joseph Jasper Stone**, who had been in the **Civil War as a Union soldier**, had been hurt during the war and got a pension. He was a **G.A.R.** out of the state **Iowa.**

He was sent to **Normal School in Nebraska** and was trained to be a teacher and learning to write poetry, stories, and the eloquent hand writing of that time. During this time he married a pastor's daughter and had three daughters and divorced soon afterward and never remarried. His daughters seemed to stay with both him and his ex wife and the girl's mother stayed in Nebraska.

He came to Oswego Kan. where his brother lived then moved to Caney where he ran the newspaper there for two years.

Joseph Jasper Stone had had **'The Caney Chronicle'** in **Caney,** had been a doctor there and was established there then decided to move to **Niotaze** and he ran' **The 'Horoscope Newspaper'** 1893 and 1894. This was the only newspaper Niotaze ever had.

He had been educated to be a **teacher** in Neb. but practiced as a **Homeopathic Doctor, taught fancy penmanship**, had a very nice **library** containing 500 books or more, he **wrote articles and stories for several magazines**, was a dedicated and vocal Republican and **G.A.R.** member, **wrote poetry and stories that were 'continued' in his newspaper, raised and sold 'fancy chickens'** His three daughters named Zoe Stone, Denton Stone and Theron Stone went to school in Niotaze and also worked on the Horoscope newspaper.

When he had the newspaper in Caney he had a section of the paper for **Civil War veterans** to write in with news and to ask questions, similar to the Dear Abby column in the 1960's.

He wanted school teachers to have free papers and offered to trade eggs, chickens, and whatever for a newspaper subscription. He wanted everyone to be up to date on the news.

While in Niotaze he traveled to Caney and Peru to visit and exchange news and he and had a hat made in Peru.

He took **Zoe and her fiancée** to be married in Sedan and the newly weds moved to **Indian Territory** afterwards.

He hired men from town to do chores for him and had them pick up many sand rocks and put them in two great big piles and the two rock piles are still there.

Born in Iowa Jan. 16, 1845 and died Oct. 10, 1920 in Niotaze in a house fire. His house was stacked and filled with magazines, articles, and his very nice library. It is said his library was prized most of all by him.

He had been in the **Civil War,** a teacher, farmer, and business man, a newspaper editor and traveled, but for the last 27 years of his life he had made Niotaze his home.

At age 71 he was laid to rest in 1920 in the **Niotaze Fairview Cemetery.**

Niotaze Churches

In 1895 **Mr. S. A. Burson** built the **Methodist Church** for
$ 1,660.00 and the two stories **Burson Hotel** both made of
limestone rock.

At this writing the **Methodist Church and the Burson Hotel** are
still standing.

There was a **Pentecostal Holiness Church** where several
attended and worshipped.

At one time they had a woman preacher named Mary Ford.

In 1877 till 1898 **The Church of Christ** had their worship
services in the **Birch Creek School** house then they moved into
their new church house in the new town of Niotaze and named
their new church '**The First Christian Church**'.

In the 1950's **Leigh and Pearl (Nance) Mathers and Nellie
Williams** were always on the church board caring to its needs.
Vern and Verna Troutman then took over the duties.

In the 1980's the church was closed and was torn down in the mid
1990's and all that is left is it's steps and sand rock foundation.

See The Niotaze Christian Church History.

The Sunflower State Refinery

In 1900-1903 there was a 'boom' in **oil, gas, drilling, and
production** in Chautauqua and in Southwestern Montgomery
Counties in Kansas.

Four miles west of Niotaze, Peru area oilfields were especially
productive.

They had the **oil** and **gas** but they needed a **market** for it.
Kansans wanted to control their oil and gas themselves.
Standard Oil and others had a monopoly driving up and
controlling prices.

Standard Oil went to **Oklahoma** securing their oil production for
their refineries and built lines for shipment instead of sending it by
train bypassing **Kansas.**

H.B. West of Peru, Kansas was **President of the Chautauqua
County Oil Producers Association.** Several men who had oil was
coming to him and he and several men called for a meeting in
Topeka, Kansas

It is said the train cars were fully packed with men from
Chautauqua County Kansas going to Topeka then packed returning
home.

H.B. West presided over the meeting in Topeka and was made **President** at that meeting and he appointed men to work with him and they set up **rules** and **laws** and most of them are still used today.

They decided to set up **Independent Refineries** and using prisons to furnish workers for refineries but that was determined to be illegal.

They decided to build a refinery in every town district that was producing oil and gas.

It 1905 it is said the erection of **The Sunflower State Refinery** was the most important event in the town's history.

It was built north of town near where the two rail roads were located.

The oil was shipped in tank cars and there was a building where **wooden barrels** were made. They were made and filled with a special kind of **lubricating oil** and shipped in boxcars.
Paraffin was also made.

During the days of the refinery, some people say there was a population of around 500 people and others say around 1000.

(In 1905 157 pupils were enrolled in the Niotaze School.)

In 1905 these refineries were built and ready for business.

1. Cherryvale Refinery Company in Cherryvale.
2. Paola Refining Company in Paola, Kansas
3. Standard Asphalt and Rubber Company in Independence, Kansas
4. Uncle Sam Refining Company in Cherryvale, Kansas
5. Superior Refining Co. in Longton, Kansas
6. The Sunflower State Oil Refinery in Niotaze, Chautauqua, County, Kansas. (It was close to the two rail roads)

Between 1904 and 1910 there were 16 refineries built; in Atchison, Caney, Chanute, Cherryvale, Coffeyville, Erie, Humbolt, Independence, Kansas City, Longton , Niotaze, Paola, and Petrolia. One of these was the National Refining Co. which still exists as Coffeyville Resources in Coffeyville.

A group first thought of building a State owned refinery.
They chose **Niotaze** because of it's location near the **two railroads** coming near it
And they thought to build a **satellite state prison** at Niotaze also to provide a ready source of inmates to operate the refinery.
Even though the Kansas State Prison in Lancing commercially

used prisons in operating coal mines, the state courts ruled that a **state owned and operated refinery was illegal along with using prisoners.**

In 1904 the **Richardson-Mott Company** contracted to build a small refinery at Niotaze financed by stockholders in Rochester New York. It was ready for use in 1905.

The plant was operated under the name of **The Sunflower State Refining Company of Niotaze, Kansas.**

The small company did not bring in the money the investors had hoped for with management stripping off the top leaving the investors with little. With the thoughts of going bankrupt they found a lady named **Miss Hermena Kaessmann from Rochester, N.Y.** who had been a school teacher and at present held the office of 'Principal of Schools'. She also invested and was a financial advisor and had $200.000.00 of her own.

Miss Hermena Kaessman bought the Richardson-Mott stocks to the refinery making herself a share holder.

Some of her lady friends also had bought stocks in the venture.

The next four years of her life was dedicated to rebuilding the refinery into a profit making enterprise.

She walked the 35 acres studying and taking notes of the machines, the pipes, and everything associated with it and she took away the middle man.

When she took over the refinery it had a market value of $30,000.00, was $14,000.00 in debt, and had $3.00 in the treasury.

The present refinery was set up to make kerosene and fuel oil which sold at a lower price than lubricating oil and paraffin, both high profit products. She set the refinery to produce those instead.

Then she had the plant expanded across the road. The plant's profits were $5,000.00 per month. She had storage barrels to hold 1,400 barrels of oil.

The plant had grown from an initial investment of $30,000.00 to $369.000.00 without any cost to the stockholders. The daily production capacity had risen from 250 barrels per day to 1,500 barrels per day with an additional 600 barrels per day coming from the new lubricating plant.

Today (2014) it is said to be the **largest oil refinery in the state** at that time and it was the **only one ever ran by a woman!!!**

She had several hungry male enemies who jealously coveted getting her out of the way by any means possible so they themselves could reap the rewards of her tireless work and efforts and take control of the refinery themselves.

Miss Hermena Kaessmann finally did resign and turned the refinery over to her adversaries. The plant started with a male manager, then after Miss Kaessmann , to operate under 3 more male managers, each time changing the name while the refinery was deteriorating due to self greedy management.

'The Sunflower State Refining Company.

Here is a list of names it went under, each time under new management.

1. The Sunflower State Refining Company 1905--1912
2. Miller Refining Company 1912
3. Niotaze Refining Company 1913--1915
4. Schock Refining Company 1915
5. O.K. Refining Company 1916—1919

I found a very small picture saying 'Fire at the refinery' and it does not state when. Refineries catching fire were a great threat to the industry and surrounding areas.

With natural reduction of oil the deteriorating refinery was shut down on 1916 and was headed for bankruptcy again and the **Carbondale Machine Co.** claimed the **'refining machine'** on site. The refinery was sold to Armistice Company and shipped to Fort Worth, Texas.

It is written that the refineries were expensive to build, run, and repairs were expensive to fix. Also, ever so often they had to be updated to comply with federal regulations.

In 1942 the land where the **Sunflower State Refinery** had made it's home was owned by O.L. Dikeman and was sold to Benton J. Flesher in 1946.

Miss. Hermena Knessmann had rebuilt, expanded, and made sure there were no leaking lines. Everything was pristine. I have found and written down that some wastes were being cleaned up through the 95 years later after closing.

Jan. 2009 F.F.R.A. tested the surface soil and the refinery exceeded residential R.S.K. standards.

May 2010 3000 yards of waste material was found.

Nov. 2010 Residential Action- children exposed to refinery

waste and impacted soil.

March 2011 Excavated and encased 2,321 cubic yards from 6 acres. Gas well plugged.

Aug. 2011 Ground is safe. No further action needed.

On one map only 3 refineries remain in operation in Kansas. One is 'The Coffeyville Resources in Coffeyville, Kansas.

1905-1916

During the time **The Sunflower State Refinery** plant operated there were three grocery stores, a meat market, ice house, an ice cream parlor, drug store, dentist and doctor's offices, greenhouse, picture gallery, theater, barber shop, livery stable, pool hall, two train depots, a grain elevator, cotton gin, stockyards, and 3 churches.

The **Niotaze Bank** was built in 1909 which was a prosperous institution in the community until the closing of the' **The Sunflower State Refinery'**. It was bought by the **Caney Valley National Bank**. The bank building was torn down for it's bricks. It is said that at that time it is the only time the vault had been cracked even though there had been **robberies** and the **robbers** had tried to crack it but never could.

It is said after the refinery closed, the population and businesses dwindled and the community went back to being a **farming community. .**

2014

Now there is the **Post Office** that is housed in one of the first buildings in Niotaze. It was a **General Store** owned by **W. T. Williams** and run by **W. D. Nance.** The sign on the west side of the store building says **W. T. Williams and Son.** The son died at an early age and members of the family ran it for many years. The last family member was **Pearl (Nance) Mathers** and her and her husband **Leigh Mathers** ran the store and post office. In later years **Leonard and Phyliss Farner** took over operating the store and post office.
Inside the store was completely remodeled and the grocery part taken out and it is a **Post Office only** now.

The **General Store with Post Office** also was the place where the **Odd Fellows #438** and **D.O.R. #286** met upstairs on the second floor. Several of the ladies and fellows of the area belonged to it.

In the 1960's there were three businesses: two grocery stores, **Mathers grocery store with the Post Office** and **James and Oceana Greers grocery store** that at one time had **sold gasoline** in front of their store, and **Bob Henderson's gas station with a garage** which was where the men congregated to swap the news and gossip.

There was a Niotaze **4 H Club** and an **Extension Homemakers Club** for the ladies. In the early 1970's I was the reporter for the **E.H.U.** group and sent their news in along with the town's weekly news to the Sedan Times Star and the Caney Chronicle.

J, J. Stone had the only city newspaper in 1893 and 1894.

There were no more newspapers but people would take turns contacting area families asking for any news they might have and would send it to the Sedan Times Star in Sedan, Ks. and to The Caney Chronicle in Caney, Kans. and both papers would send them a free copy of their paper as payment plus postage stamps. I was one of the several who collected news. The town no longer has their news reported.

Robert Rayl, a Federal Writer

Newton Rayl had attended the Niotaze school and so did his sons Wilber and Robert. They were hard working farmers.

I found on the internet that **Robert Rayl** had been a **Federal Writer for the Kansas Works Project Administration or W.P.A.**

Submitted by Robert Rayl:

Box 3 F.F.3. Title County: Chautauqua County Description

Topic: Unwritten History of Chautauqua County.
The Birth of Niotaze, Pioneers of '71 (1871) History of Chautauqua, County.

Topic: Industry and Commerce
Leading Manufactures, Natural Resources, Plants and Natural Resources, Plants and Factories of Sedan City

Topic Points of Interest: Chautauqua Springs, County Courthouse, Deer Creek Lake, Sedan City Hall, Elgin High

School, Niota Elementary School, Peru High School, Sedan High School.

Topic: Accommodations: Sedan Tourist Accommodations. Federal Writers Project Records for Kansas of the Work Project Administration. W.P.A.

William A. and Bonita (Bates) Patterson

William A. 'Bill' was a **Contract Officer for the Chautauqua and Montgomery County Soil and Water Conservation District**.
William was **Director of the Niotaze School Board.**
William was on the board of directors of the Fairview Cemetery.

Bill Patterson Jr.

Oct. 2, 1933- Sept. 2, 2013

William Bates Patterson was born William and Bonita Bates Patterson in Niotaze, Kansas and went to school there and attended the Caney High School. He went on to Kansas State University and got a degree in agricultural engineering.

He volunteered for the U.S Army and became a paratrooper with the 11th. Airborne Division at Fort Campbell, Kentucky.

For 25 years he worked for the U.S.D.A Soil Conservation Service in Burlington, Dodge City, and Salina, Kansas ending his career as their Nebraska Assistant State Soil Conservationist

He served as President of the Caney School Board, served on the Sedan Watershed Board, and also served on several committees at the Caney Methodist Church.

Bill was also active in the 4-H club with his children.

After retiring Bill and his wife Peg built a home on their farm in Southeast Kansas in the area he grew up in and became a farmer.

He like organizing hayrides, fishing, hunting, and spending time with his family and friends.

Benny Patterson

April 2, 1938-Dec.13, 1982

Benny Patterson was born April 2, 1938 to Bill and Bonita Bates Patterson and lived his whole life in Niotaze, Kansas. He attended grade school at Niotaze and graduated from Caney High School. For many years he was a professional winning many national awards in calf roping.

Bennie married Mary Hinkle and together they had three children, Justin, Jed, and Joannie.

Bennies parents set aside a large room to display his many winning trophies. Boniita invited me in and it was awesome. On a saddle rack set a beautiful saddle he had won.

The Western Horseman Magazine would have articles in their magazine telling of his horsemanship, his skills, and winnings

He was injured in an accident that left him virtually paralyzed.

Benny attended the **Niotaze Christian Church**.

Harry Dean Ledbetter

Aug. 26, 1944-May 24, 1953

Harry Dean was a son of Sam and Bandy Ledbetter and was a life long member of the town of Niotaze..

The town was sadden when Harry Dean Ledbetter drowned while swimming with friends and family. He was missed by family, friends, and at school by his teachers and classmates.

Jed Patterson

July 27, 1964- April 16, 1969

Jed Patterson was born July 27, 1964 to Bennie and Mary (Hinkle) Patterson.

He had a great love for horses and at four years old he had his own Shetland pony. The pony was dappled brown with a white main and tail.

He was always with his father Bennie riding their horses and enjoying each other's company. At Niotaze they would ride by in the evenings, Jed ahead on his pony wearing his white cowboy hat with father Bennie riding his horse close behind him. They would both always wave as they passed by.

April 16, 1968 they rode horse back to a pasture owned by Bill Patterson Jr. who lived in Salina to check out the pasture and Jed's pony slide into the pond and Jed lost his life. He was four years old.

They had a home viewing as Mary his mother set close.

His sister is Joann who is in the second grade and a brother Justin who is in the third grade.

Bill Sr. and Bonita Patterson was his grandparents and his maternal grandmother was Joann Hinkle and great grandmother was Mrs. Crayton Lookout of Pawhuska, Ok.

Bill Patterson Jr. was his uncle, and **Rosalie (Erwin) Wahl, the first woman Minn. High court justice, was his third cousin.**

Rosalie (Erwin) Wahl

She spent her childhood in Niotaze and graduated from Caney High School in 1942.

She was first female Supreme Court Justice in Minnesota in 1977. She retired in 1994 at age 70.

She is revered in Minn. for not only being the first female on that state's high court but for her legal opinions that opened doors to women, minorities, and persons with mental disabilities.

Growing up in Niotaze she and her brother Billy Erwin lived with their grandparents Claude and Effie Patterson on the family farm south of Niotaze in the 1930s.

She attended the University of Kansas where she was studying journalism and became interested in the plight of minority students on campus and desegregation.

Rosalie Wahl had loaned photographs, newspaper clippings, and plaques to the Caney Museum.

She attended the Birch Creek School outside of Niotaze which was consolidated with the Niotaze School system in 1946.

She is a cousin of Bill sr., second cousins with Bill jr. and Bennie Patterson, and third cousin to Jed, Justin, and Joannie Patterson.

Mrs. Wahl is living her retirement out in Lake Elmo, Minn.

She retired in 1994 at age 70.

Emily Haddad, a corporate lawyer turned film maker is from Stillwater, Minn. came to Sedan and Caney to do research on the family.

E. H. U.

1970's

Lottie Haines
Thelma Henderson
Ladonna Henderson
Lila Ferrell
Grace Rinck
Mary Carter
Edith Carter
Bethene Snider
Betty Smith
Ida Gragg
Wauneta Hoard

****

4 H

Edwin Bowman
Tammy Bowman
Frank Farner
Justin Patterson

Memories of School Days: Looking Back

I found pictures of Crit Nance and his wife with two other
unidentified couples saying they were share holders in
The Sunflower State Refinery.
Also a picture of Crit Nance as coach of the basket ball girl
team of Niotaze School.

Community Meetings: People would come in and
visit and get acquainted and visit each other and
talk about crops, jobs, family, etc. as they ate the
snacks that were served.

Box Suppers

Plays on stage

Ball games-boys and girls

Basket Ball games-boys and girls

Took us to watch Christian Movies at Caney
Theater 'The Robe' and others.

Take us on hikes with a sack lunch and we
collected pretty fall leaves for our classroom.
One time our hike took us north of town to the
railroad and we walked past the The Sunflower
State Refinery site where it had been and
seen some old foundation that had been left
behind.

We were taken to Caney by bus to ride the Stream Line Train to
the Independence Park and Zoo with our sack lunches. We ate our
lunches, played in the park and visited the zoo then we came back
to school.

We rode in the school buses to **Medicine Lodge, Kansas** to a
Wild West Show to watch covered wagons and lots of horses,
Indians, and cowboys, blazing guns and flying arrows while we
smelled the smell of gunpowder filling the air!

Bill Patterson brought several Indian made items
to class to show them and tell us about the Indians.
He passed the items around so we could look
closely at them and the tanned hides were so soft

On trips going to and coming back on the bus we would all sing songs. I remember one song especially we would sing and act out is:

The Acorn Song

I'm an acorn small and round laying on the cold cold ground.
Everybody steps on me that is why I'm cracked you see! I'm a nut!
I'm a nut! I'm a nut!!
Took myself to the picture show and seated myself on the very
front. Put my arms around my waist and got so fresh I slapped my
face! I'm a nut! I'm a nut! I'm a nut!

I sang it to my nieces, nephews, my own children and
grand children and acted it out and they loved it!!

I'm a Little Tea Pot----

I'm a little tea pot short and stout
Here is my handle
Here is my spout
When I get a little steam up hear me shout!
Pick me up and pour me out!

---

99 Bottles of Beer

99 bottles of beer on the wall
99 bottles of bear
take one down and pass it around
99 bottles of beer on the wall

98 bottles of beer on the wall
99 bottles of beer
take one down
pass it around
98 bottles of beer on the wall

97 bottles of beer on the wall
97 bottles of beer
take one down
pass it around
97 bottles of beer on the wall

(And the song continues until it gets to one only bottle of beer!)

There were several others but after almost 50 years we can not remember them!!

Impact of Consolidation of Schools

In 1966 the **Niotaze School** was consolidated with Caney Valley School in Caney, Kansas, Montgomery County.

The school buses picked up the children at their homes and took them home. They children did not get to stop at the stores and filling station to visit and buy candy and pop.

Mather's Grocery Store stopped selling groceries and the Bob Henderson filling station quit selling gasoline and giving services such as checking oil and tires and washing wind shields.

Children grew up and left the community to find jobs and get married and wanted to be close to their children's school and the older parents moved to be closer to their children, their doctors, grocery stores, nursing homes, and service stations to buy gas.

Many of the old homes have disappeared in town. Where many houses sat are now vacant lots.

Some of those children do move back to Niotaze when they retire and it is said it is a 'retirement community.'

The families who farmed usually stays put and the farm is passed down to the children and their grandchildren and the families' generations stay together.

The **Methodist Church** that was built by a Mr. Burson has not been used for several years and is listed on the Historical Society Registry.

The First Christian Church of Niotaze was abandoned and torn down in 1997. Parts of it's steps and foundation still remains.

The Pentecostal Holiness Church was abandoned and town down several years ago.

The **Greer's Grocery Store,** a red brick, was taken down and removed. At one time Jim and Oceana sold gasoline from a pump that was in front of the store.

The Niotaze State Bank building was torn down for the red antique bricks. It's vault had never been cracked open by robbers through the years but it was cracked or opened when the building was taken down and it was removed.

The bank was built because of **The Sunflower State Refinery** and a lot of money went through it.

In 1955 while on a school field trip the class walked north of town past where **The Sunflower State Refinery** had been and some of us walked into the tall grass and seen some of the remains of the refinery.

Remembering School Days

Each morning was started with the **Flag Salute** and

The Lord's Prayer.

The Flag Salute

**I pledge the allegiance
To the flag
Of the United States of America
And to the Republic
For which it stands
One Nation under God
With Liberty and Justice for all**

The Lord's Prayer

**Our Father which art in Heaven
Hallowed be Thy name
Thy kingdom come
Thy will be done
On earth as it is in Heaven
Give us this day
Our daily bread
Forgive us our debts
As we forgive our debters
Lead us not into temptation
But deliver us from evil
For Thine is the kingdom
And the power
And the glory forever**

Amen

Art Classes

May Day 1st. We would make **mother day cards** for our mothers. We would cut flowers out of construction paper and hang them on the windows and black board.

Students would use different colors of crepe paper then wrapped it around the **flag pole.**

On a **students birthday** the mothers would bring homemade cakes and sometimes ice cream bars and ice cream sandwiches in the afternoon after last recess for a student's birthday. One game played was 'Pin the Tail on the Donkey'.

On **Easter** everyone would bringing 6 colored eggs to school and the school would have a **Easter Egg Hunt** after the last recess. April

On **Shamrock Day** we would all wear the color 'green' or we would get pinched. March

On **Thanksgiving** we would make pumpkin and turkey cutouts and tape on the windows and blackboards Nov.

Christmas- we'd cut Christmas trees and decorate them and tape them to the windows and blackboards.
Dec. We drew names and would get gifts.

January would cut **'Snow Flakes'** out of typing paper and hang them on the windows and blackboard with tape.

Feb. we would cut out **hearts** out of construction paper and decorate it with crayons colored with crayons or cut designs with typing paper and on the red hearts.

March we would made **Shamrocks cut outs from** green construction paper and tape them to windows and blackboards.

Oct. when weather was nice would cut out **leaves** of all colors, construction paper and up.

History: Keeping Our Clothes Clean

The first homesteaders would use the plant **'Yucca- Soap Weed'** which grows wild. They would grind the root to use as soap to wash their clothes with. Some would use it to wash dishes and take a baths with also.

They then learned they could burn wood for heating and cooking then take the ashes and make **Lye Soap** and use a tub full of water drawn from a well and a **'wash board'** to wash clothes. Then you would dry them on a '**clothes line'** then take them in and **starch** and **iron** them.

Then the **washing machine** came out and all you had to do was fill it with well water and put in the soap and clothes and it would wash them. After washing you would drain the wash water and replace it with fresh water and add the wet clothes. This would rinse the soapy dirty water out then you would hang them on the line to dry.

When they were dry they were gathered in and folded up or starched and ironed. Every house had a **clothes line**.

You could also use this **Lye Soap** to wash dishes and bathe with.

On wash day the lady of the house usually put on a **pot of beans** to cook so they would be ready for supper as wash day was an all day chore.

Now we have the electric washers and dryers and permanent press fabrics.

Feeding the family before Wal Mart.

Before The Sunflower State Refinery was built, Niotaze was a farming community and in harvest would hire **hay hands** or helpers for field and garden work.

Farmers had **milk cows**, usually Jersey, and Guernsey as their milk was high in fat and they had **hand cranked Cream Separators** that separated the milk and cream then put it in iron cream cans and sell it and picking up spots.

Usually farmers had chickens and would sell eggs and the roosters were used for Sunday fried chicken dinners. Killing the rooster was also the woman's job.

There were wild plum trees, blackberry bushes, and wild grapes to gather, can, and eat.

There were trees that bees built honey combs in and a farmer would watch it and gather in the wild honey with the honey comb.

The ponds and rivers held many fish and pastures held many wild rabbits to eat and the trees were full of squirrels. Then for fall one could butcher a hog, salt it down, and cut meat as needed through the winter.

Each home had a large garden and an orchard with fruit trees and a black walnut tree.

The woman of the house usually took care of the garden, canning the fruit and vegetables, killed and cleaned the chickens and fed her family and the hired help her husband had hired to help get in the crops.

The ladies usually had an 'egg business' and also sold cream and butter for household expenses. She usually also made the family clothing and would darn hats and socks for winter.

Mrs. John R. Dodson, Ruth, told she was given a large freezer for her birthday and was delighted as many fruits and vegetables she could now freeze instead of can and it was faster and easier and done away with the pressure cookers and glass jars!

Now

Now we buy our food that is already canned and prepared from grocery stores.

Now we have Microwaves.

Now we can buy already prepared food and T.V. dinners giving us time to relax in front of the television watching our favorite programs and enjoy the internet.

Jobs and Employment

Before **The Sunflower State Refinery** Niotaze was a farming community and when the refinery was shut down it returned to a farming community.

The farmers would hire 'hay hands' when needed and there were several 'cow traders' who would make money on their trading skills and they would also haul livestock to the sales for a fee when needed.

Before automobiles got so complicated with 'censors' there were men who would come out and work on cars and pickups and they were called 'shade tree mechanics'

There were men who would do carpenter work.

There was 'oil field' work for men then as now.

There was a 'green house' in Sedan that hired seasonal employment and still does.

In the 1950's and early '60's several residents were working at the Continental Can Company in Coffeyville.

Some People who made Niotaze their home over the years.

Bud and Lois Allison with Linda, Larry, and Deana.

Bob Artherton

Wayne Artherton

Charley and Ida Barnhart (Fielding) with James and brother Jim Fielding.

Mr. and Mrs. Bailey with Billy and sister.

Mr. and Mrs. Birdwell with Connie

Mr. and Mrs. Leo Boone with Leo Boone

Floyd and Ruth Bowles
(Trader)

Bill and Letha (Burris)Carter. (Retired)

George and Mary (Howard) Carter with Debra, Becky, and Mary(Fannie)

Homer and Edith Carter with Larry and Billy. (Mattoon, Ill.)

Mr. and Mrs. Fred Carra with Billy Mike and Ray

Mr. and Mrs. Carra with Doug and Kathleen

Patsy Clark with Randy and Marlyn

Mr. and Mrs. Buck Clawson with Tommy and Billy Thompson

Aaron and Hattie (Moreland) Cooper with Fanna, Fern, and Margie. (Farmer, Cattle, and Trapping).

Mr. and Mrs. Charles Chrisman with Helen and Maxine

Fred (Bud) and Wilma (Billie) Cullins with Billy, Mary, Jennie, Hank, and Jimmy. (Game Warden and Pepsi)

Fred (Bud) and Coleen Cullins with Billy and Mary.
(Disabled)

Mr. and Mrs. George and Gladys Dodson with John R. and Sara Patterson. (Farmer and University Professor)

John R. and Ruth Dodson with Becky, Susie, and Patty.
(Farmers)

R.C. and Flossie Dye with Rita, Beverly, Amy, Linda, and Randy, and Charles.(Farmers)

Mr. and Mrs. Loyd Dickey with Glenn and Norma.

Claude and Mary (Finney)Dufoe with Joann
(oil field)

Mr. and Mrs. Victor Earhart with Luella, Pauline, and
Victor jr. (Farmers)

Mr. and Mrs. Bill Ellis with Ruby (Livery Stable)

Frank and Winona Farner with Leonard, Wayne, Betty, ----

Leonard and Phyllis Farner with Frankie, Brenda,----xxxxxx
(Post Office and Farmed)

Mr. and Mrs Farris

Clyde and Lila Ferrell with Bill
(Farmers)

Clint and Georgia Finney with Katy, Susan, Timothy,
and Tommy. (Oil Field)

Mr. and Mrs. Clarence Finney with Johnny, Kyle, Harold, David,
Melvin, Mary, (Rail Road and CCC)

David Finney

Johnny Finney

Kyle Finney

Mr. and Mrs. Fiscus with Kathy and Becky

Ben and Dorothy Flesher with Susie, and Betty Louise.

Mr. and Mrs. Freeman with Hershel Freeman.

Pat Fritz with Kathy, Ed, Elizabeth, Jill,

Mr. and Mrs. Ira Fulton with Timmy

John and Ida Gragg with June Smith and Willis Smith

James and Oceana Greer with Jimmy
(Store)

Mr. and Mrs. Ira Guier
(School Bus Driver)

Mr. and Mrs. Alford Henderson with Susie
(Dozier Work)

Q.C. and Marie Henderson with Glenda and Gary.
(Farm and School Teacher)

Floyd and Lottie Haines with Johnny Haines

Ledoit and Mary Haughn with Shirley, Roger, John, and Wauneta.

Everett and Thelma Henderson with Bob Henderson

Bob and Donna (Brown) Henderson with Melissa, Robert,
(Filling Station)

Mr. and. Mrs. Jake Hess   (Farmers)

Harvey and Alma(Ledbetter) Jones(Cement Finisher)

Mr. and Mrs. Hilbert with Marie (Farmers)

George and Waunita Hoard with Ray, Roy, Danny, and Allen

William and Fanna (Cooper) Howard with Mary
(Farmers, machine shop and 'Rosie the Riveter'CCC)

Mr. and Mrs. Paul Jenkins with Jimmy, Paul, and Larry

Mr. and Mrs. Allen Kirkpatrick with Judy, Carolyn, Dianne,
Richard and Robert.(farmers)

Sam and Bandy Ledbetter with Polly, Wanda, Alma, Ronald,
Harry, --

Mr. and Mrs. Legal with Bessie

Mr. and Mrs. Lloyd with Gary Lloyd

James and Dorothy (Ledbetter) Lumley with Jimmy
(Farmer and School Teacher)

Fern Lynn (Farmer and sold milk and eggs)

Lily Lynn cooked and prepared food and put it on a wagon (chuck wagon) in her younger years and would take this out to the farm hands in the fields in the late1800's and early 1900's. Her favorite song was 'Red River Valley' She had to move from Cascade to Niotaze to be closer to her daughter Fern in the 1950's..

Mr. and Mrs. Mc Dowell with Barbara

Mr. and Mrs. Mackey with Larry and Bobby

David and Nina Maine (Retired)

Leigh and Pearl Mathers with foster children: Anna Marie Tate, Raymond Hutchinson, Ross Torson, and others. They ran the Post Office and the Store. They were overseers of The First Christian Church, and they sponsored Cookson Hills etc. They also sponsored a family from another country years ago and the family now lives in Caney.

Vilas and Clara Meadows with Dusty

Mr. and Mrs. Mielky with Geraldine(Alexander)

Beulah McMullen with Nancy Ruth McMullen
(Retired School Teacher)

Mr. and Mrs. W.D. Nance with Crit
(Store owner)

Mr. and Mrs. Crit Nance with son.
(Owned store, was coach of Niotaze Basket Ball Team, was an invester in The Sunflower State Refinery and attended the Birch Creek Church of Christ.)

Mr. and Mrs. Albert Nance with Pearl (Nance) Mathers

Bennie and Mary (Hinkle) Patterson with Jed, Joannie, and Justin. (Ranching, Rodeo Roping, and Promoting)

William and Bonita (Bates)Patterson with William, Benny, Marion. (Farm, Cattle, Soil Conservation, Director of School)

Mr. and Mrs. Paul Phillips with John, Jimmy, and Billy

Goldia Rayl-------

Newton Rayl with Robert and Wilber (Farmers)

Bob Rinck (Farmer and Postman)

Grace Rinck (Farmers)

James and Roberta Rinck with Steve. (Farmer and Beautician)

Mr. and Mrs. Pud Rou with Donald

John and Edith Rowe

Mr. and Mrs. Salsman with Margaret, Howard, and Lenora. (Farmers)

Dan and Norma Scott with Danny and Carmelita

Mr. and Mrs. Calvin Sizemore with Bev. and Carol.

Mr. and. Mrs. Marion Smith with Marylyn
(Farmers)

Neal and Betty Smith with Lanette and Brain
(General Electric and Marines)

Betty Jo Snider with Jeremy.

Joe and Bethene Snider with Ricky, Yogi, and Betty Jo.
(Oil Field Work)

Steinberg Brothers (Oil Well Drillers)

Harold and Goldena Sullivan with Mariana, Patty, and Kenneth.
(Farmers and School Teacher)

Mr. and Mrs. Tate with Mary Ann and Jr. Tate

Harold and Frances Thorne with Danny and Susie
(Farmers)

Vern and Verna Troutman with children David, Richard, Linda
and Geneva. (Farmer and CCC)

Ed and Mary (Howard)Trowbridge with Debra, Becky, and Mary.
(Martin Concrete and Social Work)

Doris Weeks with Kathy and Jeff.

Mr. and Mrs. Vode Wessner

Mr. and Mrs. W. D. Williams with Nellie Williams.
 (Farmer and Store)

Oney and Flora Wilson with Geraldine and Betty Jean, George and
Jimmy Hoard. (Farmers)